SALT LAKE CITY
TEMPLE SQUARE

MANTI, Utah
LDS TEMPLE
MORMON Miracle Pageant

THE NAUVOO TEMPLE
1846   2002

St GEORGE
LDS Temple

LEHI, UTAH
LEHI
ROLLERMILLS

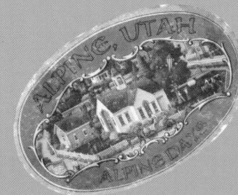
ALPINE, UTAH
ALPINE DAYS

Brigham
City, Utah
Past and Future

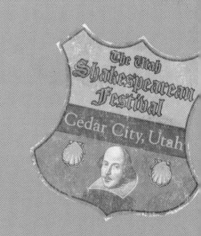
The Utah
Shakespearean
Festival
Cedar City, Utah

GREAT AMERICAN WEST RODEO
PRCA
LOGAN
UTAH

Utah's
Switzerland
INN on the CREEK
MIDWAY

Everybody climb aboard
HEBER CREEPER
RAILROAD
Heber Valley, Utah

PROVO UTAH

Lake Powell
Ticaboo, Utah

PARK CITY, UTAH

AEROSPACE MUSEUM
OGDEN, UTAH

PINE   PINE VAL
Pine Valley, Utah

Utah

FEATURING THE ART OF ERIC DOWDLE

TEXT BY WILLIAM KURTIS

ii

U

T

A

H

ISBN: 978-0-9802346-0-2

www.dowdlefolkart.com

Manufactured in China

TABLE OF CONTENTS

Artist's Acknowledgements iv

Foreward v

Journey to the Promised Land . . . 1
  Nauvoo
  Pioneer Patterns
  Mormon Wagon Train
  Sesquicentennial Wagon Train
  All Nations Shall Flow Unto It

The Right Place. 9
  Salt Lake City
  Gardner Historic Village
  The Avenues
  Salt Lake City Winter

The Valley Remembered 17
  Brigham Street
  Salt Lake City—1920
  The Lion House
  Armstrong Mansion

Building with Heart and Soul 25
  Govenor's Mansion
  Christmas in the Avenues
  City and County Building
  Salt Lake Temple

The Land of Dixie. 33
  St George
  4th in Dixie
  Green Gate Village
  Pine Valley

Cache Valley 41
  Logan Summer
  Olsen Park
  Logan Fall

Natural Wonders 47
  Bear Lake
  Lake Powell
  Delicate Arch
  Grand Canyon

Along the Way 55
  Brigham City
  Ogden
  Lehi Roller Mills

Childhood Days 63
  Hide and Seek
  School Carnival
  Camp Eagle's Nest

Resort Living 71
  Park City
  Ski Park City
  Snowed Inn
  Inn for the Evening

A Taste of the Alps. 79
  Heber City
  Midway
  Gingerbread House

Off the Beaten Path 87
  Alpine Summer
  Alpine Christmas
  Manti

Happy Valley. 95
  Provo
  Brigham Academy
  Storytellers

Fun and Thanksgiving. 103
  Thanksgiving Point
  Electric Park
  Golf at Thanksgiving Point
  Farm Country

Beyond Utah's Borders 109

Author's Note. 112

Acknowledgements

My desire in compiling this book is to tell the story of our great state. In so doing I would like to thank all those who made this possible: to my parents for not stopping at nine kids, to my wife for her love and never ending patience, to Rudy Gunter who refrained from kicking me out of art class, to Lane Beattie, president of the Utah Chamber and his wife Joy for all of their support and for providing the forward for this book, Wayne Elggren for taking a chance on a starving artist, the Winwood family for good advise and support, and Wendy Hemingway for being the heart and soul of Dowdle Folk Art. And to all those (Mark) who have laid down cold hard cash to keep me living indoors . . . thank you! And of course to William Curtis, for providing the text.

Eric Dowdle

FOREWORD

F A PICTURE PAINTS A THOUSAND WORDS, THEN JUST TURNING THROUGH THESE PAGES WILL BRING VOLUMES OF MEMORIES, EXPERIENCES, AND PLEASURES TO YOUR HEART AND MIND.

The impressions of Utah will flood into your consciousness like a warm and familiar blanket representing all that is good.

Eric Dowdle, a preeminent American folk artist, will capture your imagination with each of these incredible works of art. His ability to inspire each of us as we reminisce about city life, country life, religious life, or just the whimsical side of our being, will provide hours of pleasure, whether in our own precious solitude or while we share our personal experiences with someone else.

Eric's talent for capturing the warmth and essence of life within each of the works of art is unprecedented. His talent brings to life vivid, colorful, and exciting viewscapes, reminding us of what is good and beautiful in this world. He has taken years of research and embodied it within the framework of each masterpiece he paints.

As parents we have taken the opportunity to share these exciting treasures with our family. We have done this both as a way to teach our children and grandchildren about the history of this great country and to share the beauty of a unique art form.

For Eric to share so many of these treasures in one incredible volume is a rare and heartfelt gift to his home state. Whether it is Logan, Salt Lake City, St. George or one of the many other cities or sites we love, this compilation of the best of Utah will bring a flood of sweet memories and tender feelings.

From a grateful state, we say "Thank You." Eric has contributed to the betterment of Utah. You will find within these pages the inspiration and appreciation of Utah at its best. Let your journey begin.

Joy Beattie
Lane Beattie
  President, Salt Lake Chamber of Commerce
  Former President, Utah State Senate

 # JOURNEY TO THE PROMISED LAND

"We would esteem a territorial government of our own as one
of the richest boons of earth, and while we appreciate the
Constitution of the United States as the most precious among
the nations, we feel that we had rather retreat to the deserts...."

Brigham Young, in a letter to President James K. Polk

Nauvoo
The City of Joseph

NAUVOO *MEANS "BEAUTIFUL" IN HEBREW. WHAT HAD BEEN AN EMPTY BLUFF ON THE ILLINOIS SIDE OF THE MISSISSIPPI* became the fastest-growing city on America's frontier. Where bluffs overlook the horseshoe bend of the stately river, springs trickled down the rolling hills saturating the swampy flatlands.

Confident they could reclaim the lands, the city fathers bought tracts on both sides of the river; they plotted wide boulevards and square blocks uncharacteristic of typical western settlements.

Nauvoo would serve as a pattern for the grid plots of Mormon settlements throughout Utah and the western states. Nauvoo became a prototype community for Mormon settlement. The Pioneers built from the raw materials and natural resources found in any area that they were called to "build up to the Lord."

Artist's Note

I visited Nauvoo right after the great Mississippi Flood of 1993. All roads in and out of Nauvoo had just opened up. My family and I were the first tourists Nauvoo had seen in weeks. The reception of the tour guides and the townspeople made my research experience unforgettable. It was hard to leave in the end. For the first time in my life, I had a small understanding of how difficult it must have been for my ancestors to do the same.

PIONEER PATTERNS

Artist's Note

In tribute to the sacrifice and achievements of the first Latter-Day Saints, the *Pioneer Patterns* quilt was designed to depict the early days and events of the church. Many people have discovered deep symbolic references and hidden meanings that would cause people to believe the artist has wisdom and intelligence beyond his years. This is a debate I refuse to engage in.

THERE ARE AS MANY PIONEER STORIES AS THERE ARE STITCHES IN A HANDSEWN QUILT.

Each thread in the tapestry tells a narrative of hardship and determination. An advance pioneer company of 144 men, three women, and two children led the trek to the West. Like many who were to follow, the party brought a variety of trailblazing abilities to the task.

The party included mechanics, teamsters, hunters, frontiersmen, carpenters, sailors, accountants, bricklayers, blacksmiths, wagon makers, lumbermen, joiners, dairymen, stockmen, millers, and engineers.[1]

The pioneers blazed trails and surveyed routes that ten companies would follow to the Great Basin. The route would eventually guide subsequent settlers to Oregon and California, and chart the course of the Transcontinental Railway that would connect the arid Great Plains to the West Coast. The pioneers were seeking refuge

beyond the frontiers of known civilization, hardly aware of the lasting impact their efforts had on the building of a nation.

On Wednesday, July 21, 1847, Orson Pratt and Erastus Snow ascended Donner Hill and caught their first good view of the Salt Lake Valley. They "could not refrain from a shout of joy," Pratt recorded. Later that day, they briefly explored the valley before rejoining their company's wagon train in Emigration Canyon.

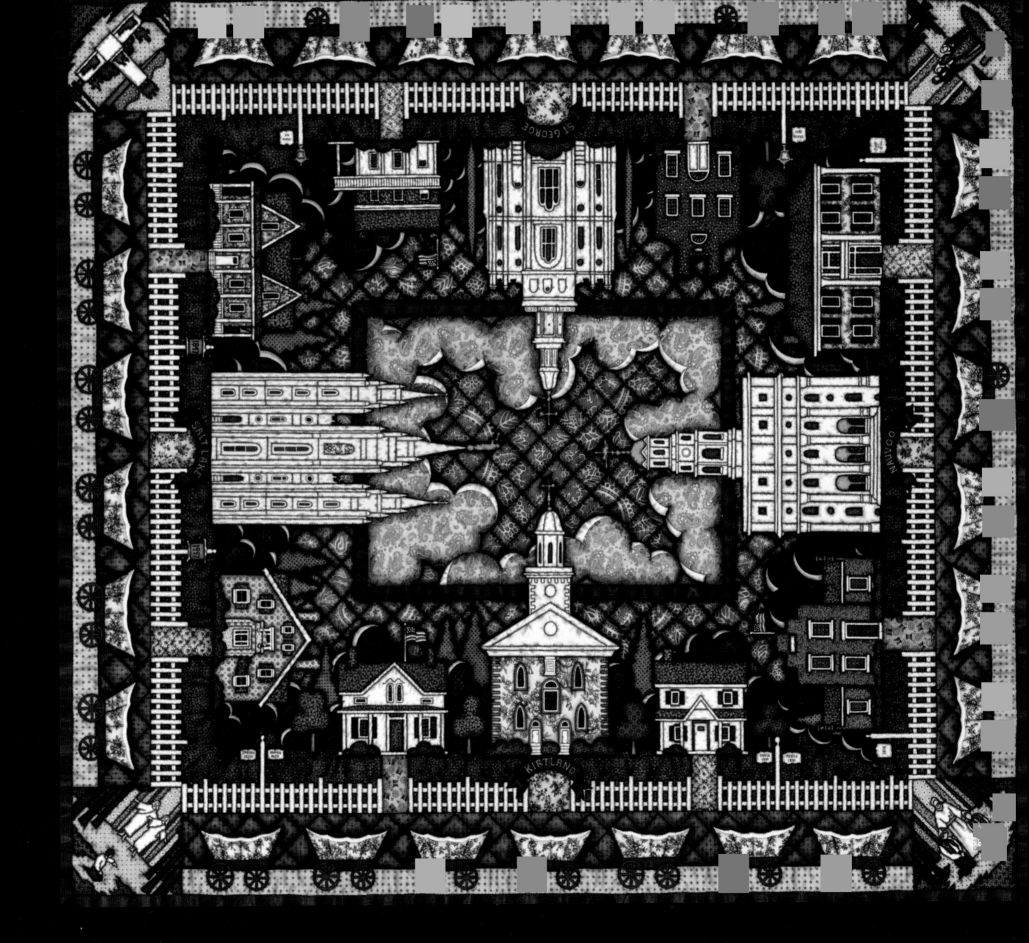

MORMON WAGON TRAIN

Artist's Note

Like most artists, I go on location for all of my paintings. Historical pieces are always a challenge because I have to see things as they once were—not necessarily as they are now. As I drove across the North Platte area, I imagined the Saints with the backdrop of a barren terrain. Long before civilization and corn covered the landscape, the Nebraska horizon must have seemed endless.

On the following day, the first Mormon wagons lumbered into the valley. From the mouth of Emigration Canyon the pioneer company moved in a southwesterly direction and then turned almost due west. Oxen and wagons beat a path through thick stands of grass over six feet high. Thomas Bullock compared walking through the grass to wading.

When the wagons arrived at the north bank of Parley's Creek, they decided to stop: the site was, in Bullock's words, "bare enough for a camping ground, the grass being only knee deep, but very thick." Nine horsemen led by Orson Pratt devoted the remainder of the day to exploring the northern portion of the valley, and at length determined that the most promising site for farming lay along City Creek, two miles directly north of their temporary encampment.

In 1997, in celebration of the sesquicentennial of the Mormon Pioneer trek of 1847, a total reenactment of the western migration of the saints took place. Authentic wagons were built; participants were chosen and outfitted with pioneer clothing. Everything was designed to replicate the event exactly as it occurred 150 years earlier.

SESQUICENTENNIAL WAGON TRAIN

This modern trek was scheduled to follow the course, dates, and miles per day of the original pioneers. The main differences would be that, hopefully, a few of the dangers of the previous trip would be eliminated, and this group would not be hunting and killing wildlife for food.

A complete book could be written about this adventure; in fact I think there already have been multiple volumes published. There were many amazing similarities, and of course, distinct contrasts found between the two trips. Perhaps the biggest difference between the two events was that on July 24, 1847 the saints entered a desolate and lonely valley with very little welcome from anyone. They then had to go right to work just to be able to survive the impending fall and winter.

In contrast, the 1997 wagon train arrived to the adulation of a huge supportive crowd and celebration. Despite the differences, the participants in the Sesquicentennial Wagon Train certainly received a better understanding of the original trials of those pioneers they chose to honor.

Artist's Note

The entire state celebrated the sesquicentennial commemoration of the pioneers. Every activity was drenched in nostalgia and fun. It was a perfect time to be a folk artist and a really great time to be in Utah. To capture the reenactment of the pioneers, I traveled to Evanston, Wyoming in July to see the Sesquicentennial Wagon Train as they recreated the event. In the middle of the summer, it was 28-degrees at five in the morning. This may have been one of the reasons the Saints didn't make Wyoming their permanent home!

ALL NATIONS SHALL FLOW UNTO IT

"I cannot help being here...we are in the valleys of the mountains, where the Lord directed me to lead the people. The brethren who are in foreign countries desire to gather to the gathering-place of the Saints, and they have to come to Great Salt Lake City. "

—*Brigham Young*

Artist's Note

In 2003, Lane Beattie, President of the Salt Lake Chamber, comissioned a painting to be awarded to one of Utah's most prominent citizens, Gordon B. Hinckley, President of the Church of Jesus Christ of Latter-day Saints. The painting was to honor his life and the contributions he has made to the downtown landscape of Salt Lake City. You can find many historic moments from the lives of President and Marjorie Hinckley throughout this painting.

# THE RIGHT PLACE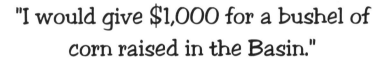

"I would give $1,000 for a bushel of
corn raised in the Basin."

Jim Bridger, on the potential of raising
any crop in the Salt Lake Valley

SALT LAKE CITY

A S BRIGHAM YOUNG LOOKED WEST OVER THE VALLEY TO THE GREAT INLAND SEA, HE EXCLAIMED, "IT IS ENOUGH. THIS IS THE RIGHT PLACE. DRIVE ON."

On July 24, 1847 Brother Brigham led the first group of exhausted Latter-Day Saints into the valley. It was probably a great relief for any parent in the group who had to endure, "Are we there yet?" for over two months and 1000 miles.

Just two days after their arrival, Brigham Young climbed to the top of a hill, now called Ensign Peak, at the north end of the valley. It was from there he looked down and located the spot where the temple would be built. The saints set out to build a structure that would last 1000 years. The Salt Lake Temple took 40 years to complete.

Located next to the Temple is the Tabernacle, home of the Mormon Tabernacle Choir. It was the location of the semi-annual General Conferences of The Church of Jesus Christ of Latter-day Saints for 132 years. The structure was an architectural wonder in its day and beyond. Frank Lloyd Wright dubbed the Tabernacle as "one of the architectural masterpieces of the country and perhaps the world."

Brigham Young founded The University of Deseret, later renamed the University of Utah. The Utah "U" on the eastern hill above the campus is over 100 feet high and is traditionally lit up after athletic victories.

Artist's Note

I believe that every city has a heart, and the heart of Salt Lake City is Temple Square. Not only is it the historical center, but also the geographical reference point for the entire valley. Through the effort of countless gardeners, Temple Square really comes alive in the spring. I wanted this painting to capture enough of that beauty to inspire everyone to come and see the real thing.

"As was common to the technology of the period, Archibald Gardner's gristmills were built without nails. Wooden pins and mortises were used instead. All shafts, bearings, cog wheels, etc. were of wood..."

—Becky Bartholomew

Artist's Note

Visiting Gardner Historic Village is like walking into a life-sized folk painting. The quaint buildings and old-fashioned shops each seem to have their own story to tell. My kids like to visit the candy store first and then carry their little brown bags full of sweets from shop to shop. I am grateful that a place like this exists for them.

GARDNER HISTORIC VILLAGE

IN 1853, ARCHIBALD GARDNER BUILT A SAWMILL ALONG THE JORDAN RIVER ON THE SITE THAT IS NOW GARDNER HISTORIC VILLAGE. IN 1877, THE SAWMILL BECAME A FLOUR MILL AND A BUSTLING CENTER OF INDUSTRY THAT INCLUDED A MATTRESS FACTORY, BROOM FACTORY, BLACKSMITH SHOP, AND GENERAL STORE.

More than a century later, this mill is the home of Gardner Historic Village, Country Furniture and Gifts, and Archibald's Restaurant. The buildings around the mill consist of restored cabins, houses, and buildings—each one housing theme shops offering quilts, art, gifts, collectibles, furniture, and much more.

Archibald was born in Scotland in 1814, emigrated to Canada, and then to the U.S. after joining The Church of Jesus Christ of Latter-day Saints. He was one of the original settlers of Utah in 1847—the year the first wave of pioneers arrived in the Salt Lake Valley.

Over his lifetime, Archibald has built Thirty-Six mills: Twenty-Six in Utah, Five in Wyoming, Two in Idaho, and Six in Canada.

Archibald also owned a parcel of land in Bingham Canyon, located southwest of his flour mill on the Jordan River. He eventually sold this land, and it was subsequently developed into the Bingham Canyon Mine, the third largest copper mine in the United States.

Gardner Historic Village with the original mill is a fitting monument to Archibald Gardner and all of his contributions to Utah.

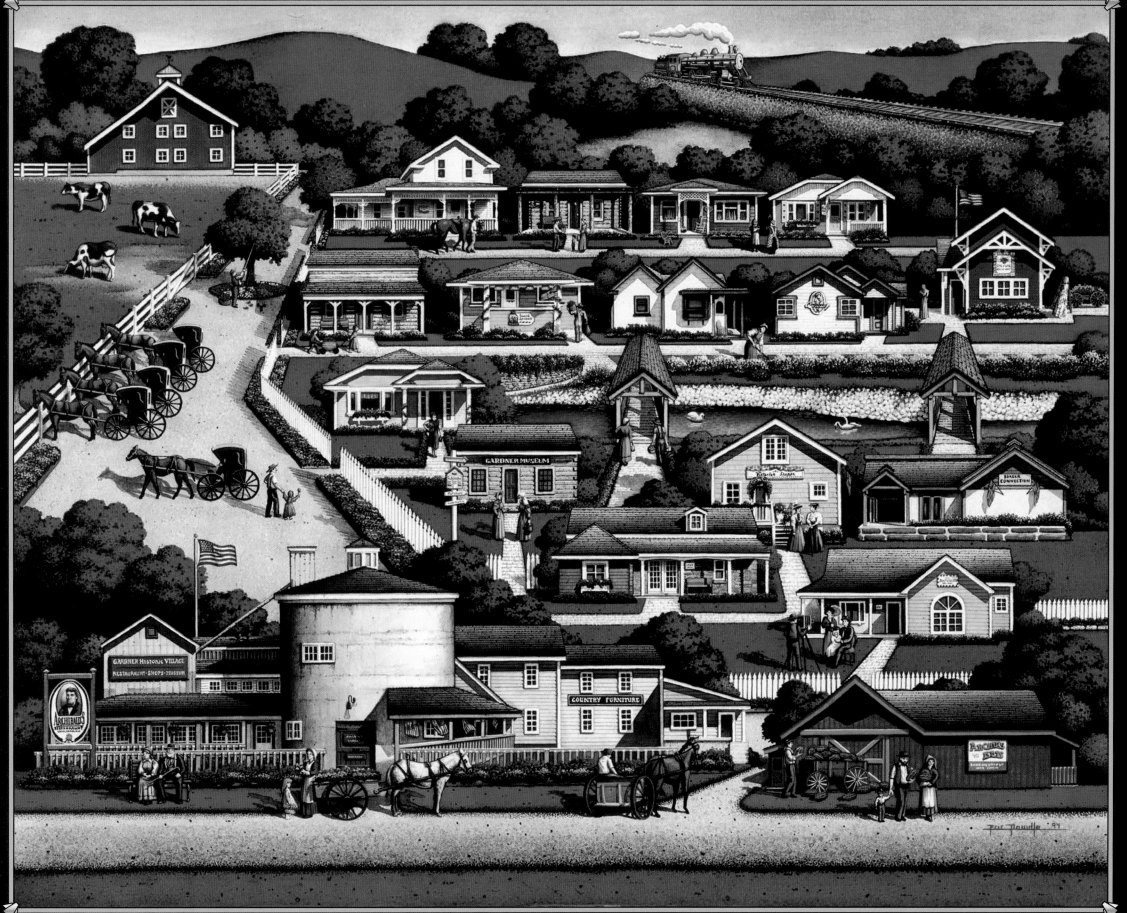

THE AVENUES

The Avenues are proof that civilization came west and settled in Salt Lake City.
—David Morse

Artist's Note

When I moved from New England to Salt Lake City the Avenues were a welcome site which reminded me of all the older homes in the east. As I drove through the neighborhood the right homes to paint seemed to call out to me. I knew then that folk art could flourish in the west.

THE AVENUES, AS THEY'RE KNOWN TODAY, WERE A DEVIATION FROM THE ORDERLINESS OF SALT LAKE CITY STREETS.

Brigham Young had originally planned the city with exactly square, ten-acre blocks separated by streets wide enough to turn an ox team around without backing up—evidence of the pioneers' practiced rationality.

Originally, everyone was to live in the city on one-and-a-quarter-acre plots and commute to their farms each day. However, the Avenues were created on the benches of the Wasatch Mountains for modern city dwellers, not the urban farmers who lived below.

The Avenues are a set of streets that climb up the steep mountain slope just northeast of Temple Square. Developed mainly after 1850, the Avenues were a real estate development carved out of the mountainside with individual lots flattened into stair-steps climbing uphill. The blocks were smaller because the houses were not intended to have large gardens like the houses in the center of the city.

The original settlers of Salt Lake City had begun a network of canals and ditches for irrigation throughout the original city. However, this network didn't bring water to the Avenues until after the turn of the century. Water had to be hauled up the slopes for everyday use.

Originally, all the streets in the Avenues had descriptive names. North-south streets were named for trees, and east-west streets had names like *Fruit, Garden, Bluff,* and *Wall*. But in the 1880s the north-south streets were given their current alphabetical designations—A Street through V Street (although V was turned into Virginia Street.) The east-west streets were renamed as numbered *Avenues* after 1907—such as 1st Avenue and 2nd Avenue.

The Avenues contain a rich architectural heritage. Many of the homes were designed from the most popular styles of their day. Taking a leisurely walk through the Avenues will treat you to styles such as Gothic Revival, Second Empire, Victorian Eclectic, Queen Anne, Shingle Style, several Period Revival styles, as well as Foursquare, and Bungalows.

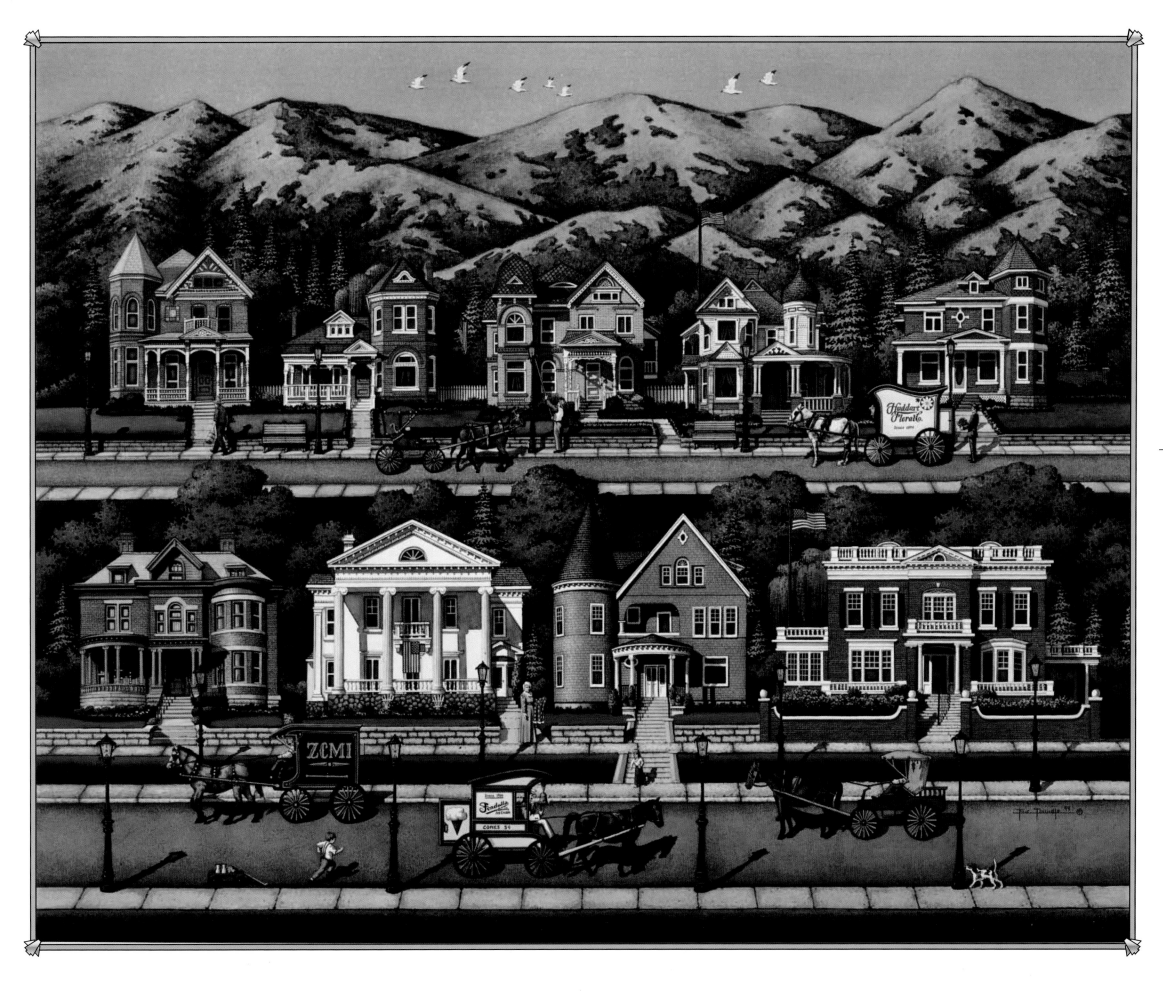

SALT LAKE CITY WINTER

THE SALT LAKE CITY WINTER OLYMPICS OF 2002 BROUGHT THE WORLD TO THE TOP OF OUR BELOVED MOUNTAINS.

The growth brought by the Olympics provided many lasting benefits. The Utah Olympic Park, created just for the Olympics, is now a major winter attraction. The winter of 2002 will be forever a shining moment of greatness and accomplishment in the history of Salt Lake City and the State of Utah.

Artist's Note

"The Winter Olympics were coming to Utah and soon the whole world would be looking at us. What would they think? How would they feel? Would they be impressed? Would they love it like we do? I wanted to paint something that would tell a thousand stories. I was taught in art class that less is more. While painting this tribute to the Olympics and winter sports in Utah I just couldn't stop, sometimes more is more."

THE VALLEY REMEMBERED

"History is the witness that testifies to the passing of time; it illumines reality, vitalizes memory, provides guidance in daily life and brings us tidings of antiquity."

Cicero, Pro Publio Sestio

"Life is best enjoyed when time periods are evenly divided between labor, sleep, and recreation...all people should spend one-third of their time in recreation which is rebuilding, voluntary activity, never idleness."

—Brigham Young

Artist's Note

Brigham Street was my very first Utah painting. I painted the Lion House and Beehive House to show that folk art could be done in Utah. My wife had introduced me to this style of art when I lived in New England a couple of years earlier. I could see that it worked well in an area with high ideals and a strong heritage. Utah was that place for me. I have been painting folk art ever since.

BRIGHAM STREET

BRIGHAM STREET IS NOW KNOWN AS SOUTH TEMPLE IN SALT LAKE CITY.

Sitting on South Temple, just a block north of historic Temple Square, is the Lion House on the left and the Beehive House on the right. Both were homes for Brigham Young, territorial governor and second president of The Church of Jesus Christ of Latter-day Saints.

Truman O. Angell, Brigham Young's brother-in-law and architect of the Salt Lake City temple, was also architect of both homes, which were built of adobe and sandstone taken from City Creek Canyon.

The Beehive House was completed in 1854 and gets its name from the beehive sculpture on top of the house. Brigham Young used the beehive to signify industry, and

it later became the Utah state emblem. This house was the executive mansion of the Territory of Utah from 1852 to 1855, and the official residence where Brigham Young entertained important guests. The Beehive House was restored in 1960 and is now decorated with period furniture—many pieces original to the home. It is currently an historic site open for public tours.

The Beehive House also served as the official residence of Lorenzo Snow and Joseph F. Smith, from 1898 to 1918, during the time that each served as president of The Church of Jesus Christ of Latter-day Saints.

The Lion House, completed in 1856, takes its name from the lion sculpture resting on top of the front porch. It was sculpted by another church architect, William Ward. The Lion House was restored in 1968 and remains a social center for wedding receptions, meetings, and parties. Its lower floor operates a popular restaurant.

SALT LAKE CITY — 1920

If you ever want an education on the "good ole days" of Utah you should take a stroll through the photo library at the Utah historic society. It is one of the best in the country. This is where I learned the visual history of our great state and what made possible the recreation of Salt Lake City—1920. Each building and activity in this painting was discovered while I was there. It was here that I really started to feel the spirit of Utah—both past and present.

THE LION HOUSE

Artist's Note

If you are far away from Grandma's house, the Lion House just may be a good substitute. I can drop in with my kids, just like Grandma's house, and get a great home-cooked meal. Or, as this painting suggests, it is a great place to gather for special occasions, wedding breakfasts, family reunions, etc. If you don't have a Grandma to visit, I promise, the rolls here are every bit as good as the real thing.

THE ARMSTRONG MANSION

BUILDING WITH HEART AND SOUL

"The mother art is architecture. Without an architecture of
our own we have no soul of our own civilization."

Frank Lloyd Wright

"It is an honor for our family to live in *the people's home* of Utah. I encourage all Utahns, both young and old, to come learn more about the Mansion's history and discover its beauty."

—Governor Jon Huntsman, Jr.

THE GOVERNOR'S MANSION

HOMAS KEARNS LEFT HIS FAMILY AT AGE 17 AND HEADED WEST TO SEEK HIS FORTUNE OUT WEST.

In 1883 he started working in the mines of Park City, Utah, as a mucker—the lowest paying job in the mine. However, he soon became one of the owners of the famous Silver King Mine, which made him a millionaire.

Thomas married Jennie Judge and became an influential businessman in Salt Lake City, part owner of the Salt Lake Tribune, and was elected a U.S. Senator.

In 1898, Thomas and Jennie started building a palatial home; They spared no expense to make it as lavish as possible. The home is constructed of *oolitic* limestone quarried in Manti, Utah. African and Italian marble and exotic woods from around the world were used extensively throughout. The Kearns Mansion was designed by Carl M. Neuhausen in the French *Chateaueque* style popular during that era. The mansion was completed in 1902 at a cost of $350,000.

Thomas and Jennie entertained often and lavishly, frequently hosting political and religious dignitaries. In 1903, the mansion was draped in bunting when President Theodore Roosevelt came to visit the Kearns.

Sixteen years after they moved into the mansion, Thomas died of a stroke a week after being struck by a car at South Temple and Main Streets.

Jennie continued to live in the home until 1937, when she deeded the 36-room mansion to the state of Utah. For the next several years the governors of Utah resided at the mansion during their terms of office.

A fire in December 1993 destroyed much of the mansion, which has now been fully restored to its 1902 appearance. Home to the governor and his family once again, the mansion has also re-opened to public tours. A favorite time for tours is December, when it's elaborately decorated for Christmas.

A white Christmas is typical for the Avenues. The festivities begin shortly after Thanksgiving and continue until New Years. Choirs of children, programs, pageants, plays, and parties with enough food and drink for everyone. It is a wonder any work gets done. And the decor....well what would the holidays be without that?

Artist's Note

One frosty day, a neighbor brought a gift basket to my family. One of the items happened to be a can of Stephen's Gourmet Hot Cocoa, definitely the best hot chocolate I had ever tasted. I called the company and inquired as to how long they had been in business. I was told that they had been in business since 1986. I informed them that as soon as I finished my painting of Christmas in the Avenues they would appear to be over 100 years old. We have been great friends ever since.

CITY AND COUNTY BUILDING

"True independence and freedom can only exist in doing what's right."

—Brigham Young

Artist's Note

The City and County Building is one of Utah's architectural crown jewels. I happened to run into the mayor while I was in the building doing my research. After navigating past her bodyguard, I asked her what part of the building she liked the most, the left or the right? She said she didn't lean one way or the other. I personally like the whole building.

THE SALT LAKE CITY AND COUNTY BUILDING WAS BUILT IN PART TO BE A BALANCE BETWEEN THE PREDOMINANT INFLUENCE OF THE LDS CHURCH AND THE NON-MORMON COMMUNITY.

Built by free masons, it was designed to rival the beauty and majesty of the Salt Lake Temple. Instead of the Angel Moroni at the point of the highest spire, a magnificent statue of Columbia was built at the pinnacle of the center clock tower.

The building was planned to replace the Salt Lake City Council Hall and Courthouse, both which had been built in the 1860s. It was riddled with controversy before ground was even broken. To the benefit of all, both sides eventually worked together and the City and County building has stood as a lasting monument to the continuing pioneer spirit that exists among Mormons and non-Mormons alike.

Shortly after its completion the City and County Building was the chosen location for the framing of the Utah Constitution. Eventually

Salt Lake County moved its offices from the building leaving the Salt Lake City offices in place. The name of the building stuck, however, and it still goes by that name today.

In the 1970s and 1980s the building was renovated extensively both inside and out. There had been some talk, from a cost standpoint, of replacing the building with something more modern. Fortunately, those who had a feeling for the important heritage of the building prevailed.

The old sandstone foundation was replaced with a base of steel and rubber to better withstand earthquake damage. Some of the statues that had been removed after the 1934 earthquake were refurbished and replaced. By the time the renovation was complete, Salt Lake City had a masterpiece once again to be proud of for generations to come.

THE SALT LAKE TEMPLE

The Salt Lake Temple took over 40 years to build. According to Brigham Young, that was acceptable because it was designed to stand for over 1000 years.

The temple site was chosen five years before construction actually began, only four days after the saints' arrival in the valley on July 24, 1847. During those 40 years, Utah changed from a primitive frontier settlement to a modern city with technology that allowed church president Wilford Woodruff, to mount the capstone of the tallest spire by operating the controls of an electric motor.

The Salt Lake Temple, over 100 years after its completion, is still the most recognized symbol, world wide, of The Church of Jesus Christ of Latter-day Saints.

Artist's Note

KEEP IT SIMPLE is what kept running through my mind as I contemplated how I could depict the Salt Lake Temple, a structure that has been painted thousands of times by countless artists. I wanted the Lord's house to stand strong and by itself. In a painting like this, I believe there should be very little distraction. (Perhaps there's a conference talk in there somewhere).

THE LAND OF DIXIE

"Dixie on the south has long been regarded as a
somewhat desert country, dry and unproductive.
Brethren and sisters, that is a fallacy."

Rudger Clawson

"If I didn't have to commute to Hollywood, I'd love to make St. George my home."

–Roy Rogers

Artist's Note

"Most agree when I say that there are few scenes as breathtaking as St. George's white temple set against the beautiful red rock of the city. There's no question as to why a folk artist would feel at home in a place such as this. Once you have been to St. George it's hard to get the red clay out of your soul. Who would want to anyway?"

St. George

ST. GEORGE WAS A PART OF BRIGHAM YOUNG'S GRAND VISION FOR COLONIZING THE WEST. WHILE SILK WAS BEING PRODUCED IN THE NORTH, ST. GEORGE GREW COTTON IN THE SOUTH.

The Old Cotton Mill was, at one time, the largest producing cotton factory west of the Mississippi. The factory operated for over 50 years. Eventually it couldn't compete with product brought in by rail. It is commonly believed, though, that the mill was one of the elements that held the community together.

The old courthouse features 18-inch thick interior walls made mostly from locally manufactured brick and mortar. Completed in 1876, the courthouse originally served as a jail.

The first public building constructed by the settlers was the St. George Social Hall. It was built in 1862 as a place of recreation, entertainment, and education. During the early 1900s to the mid-1920s, the Social Hall was called the "Opera House" because of the many operettas and vaudeville shows that were presented during those years.

Brigham Young's Winter Home gave him relief from the rheumatism he suffered during the cold northern Utah winters. From here he supervised the building of the St. George Temple.

The term "hotter than a firecracker" just may have been coined in St. George on the 4th of July. **"4TH IN DIXIE"** (on page 34) depicts the patriotic spirit of the souls who brave the heat of a St. George summer on this most festive day. Just like their "Dixie" counterparts in the original Thirteen colonies, the Fourth of July is a very special holiday in St. George. So wave your flag, and your fan.

But of course, with the advent of modern air conditioning, St. George today has become a destination for all those who, like Brigham Young, enjoy the year-round warmth of this oasis in the desert.

Artist's Note

Every spring, Leisure Services of St. George puts on one of the best art festivals in the country. Patrons and artists will agree it's an event that shouldn't be missed. I have done hundreds of festivals all over the country and this one is my favorite. This painting was done for that event.

GREENGATE VILLAGE

Artist's Note

"If you haven't stayed at this quaint Bed and Breakfast in St. George yet, then do yourself a favor and make your reservation now. My multiple visits have shown that no matter what time of year, you will be treated with the greatest of care. Visit Judd's store, have an old fashioned soda, and take a dip in the pool. Sleep in and go to breakfast. The perfect hostess will greet you and serve up a meal to remember."

PINE VALLEY

HIDDEN, TUCKED AWAY FROM THE HARSH, ARID DESERT IS A JEWEL IN THE HEART OF SOUTHWESTERN UTAH. IT WAS CONCEALED FROM MOST EARLY SETTLERS AND REMAINS, FOR THE MOST PART, A SECRET EVEN TODAY.

Pine Valley was first discovered when Isaac Riddle was looking for a very lost cow. As he trailed the cow higher and higher up a creek he suddenly stopped at the top of a hill. Isaac later wrote, "There stretching before me was the most beautiful sight I had ever beheld on God's green earth."

Huge pines and spruce grew down to the floor of the valley which was carpeted with dew-drenched grass waving as high as a horse's knee; aspen bordered the creek on either side of the valley. The only sign of life was the lost cow. Isaac, with two partners, purchased a lumber mill in Salt Lake City and moved it to what was soon to be known as Pine Valley.

Soon there was lumber enough to build the St. George Temple, the Tabernacle, and to supply the growing communities in Southern Utah and Nevada.

Eventually the Pine Valley residents wanted a nice church building of their own, but the community lacked a builder with experience in that kind of construction. In fact, the only person in Pine Valley who was even remotely qualified as an architect was Ebenezer Bryce—a shipbuilder from Scotland.

The Pine Valley Chapel was built in 1868 using some very unusual building techniques. It is the oldest continuously used building in the Church of Jesus Christ of Latter-day Saints—still loved and used by members today.

Pine Valley sits at an elevation of 6,000 feet and is surrounded by tall mountain peaks climbing to 10,300 feet into the sky. You can expect the temperature difference between St. George and Pine Valley to be at least 20 degrees. A stifling 100 degree day in St. George—just 30 miles away—is a much more tolerable 80 degrees in Pine Valley.

UTAH

CACHE VALLEY

"There were lots of Indians and squaws here. President Young
told us to be very kind to the Indians and feed them...."

John Clark Dowdle, on conditions of Cache Valley in 1855

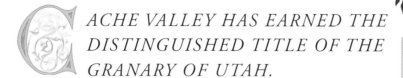

LOGAN SUMMER

CACHE VALLEY HAS EARNED THE DISTINGUISHED TITLE OF THE GRANARY OF UTAH.

Fertile fields and croplands greet the Sardine-Canyon-wary driver, and the abundance of cattle remind you that Logan is the home of Utah's famous cheese industry. Aggie Ice Cream at the Utah State "Dairy Bar" is a guilty pleasure of many a visitor to this pleasant community.

In 1855, the Utah Territorial Legislature granted Cache Valley to Brigham Young as a herd ground for his increasing numbers of cattle. The ranch they established was named the Elk Horn Ranch and became the first Mormon settlement in the valley. During the first harsh winter, 18-year-old John Clark Dowdle was credited with saving the lives of everyone there; he traveled by mule to Box Elder (Brigham City) and brought back food and supplies.

In early June of 1859 a group of Mormon settlers were sent to Cache Valley by Brigham Young. They surveyed the land to build a fort near the banks for the Logan River. By the next spring there were 100 houses in the settlement, which was named Logan after an early trapper, Ephraim Logan. The city was incorporated January 17, 1866.

The Logan Utah Temple was built by 25,000 volunteers. Rocks and timber were hauled from nearby canyons, mostly during the winter, because it was easier to haul rock by sleigh than by wagon. Women in the area were asked to make carpets for the temple because commercially-made carpets were hard to come by in Utah. They spent two months hand sewing 2,000 square feet of carpet. The temple was dedicated in May 1884 by Church President John Taylor.

In 1941, while on vacation, Edwin Gossner found the ideal location with climate and elevation closely resembling that of his native Switzerland—Logan, Utah. He built, what was at the time, the largest Swiss cheese factory in the world. Today, the seventh generation carries on the family tradition at the same homestead that has been a part of their family heritage for all these years.

Artist's Note

"Putting friends and neighbors in my paintings has always been fun for me to do. A few subliminal messages from time to time will find their way onto the canvas. I can't give away all my secrets, but if you happen to be looking at the Logan painting and have an unexplainable urge to cheer for BYU, I'm not responsible."

"Logan is very cold, but a beautiful area as well. The people are much warmer than the weather."

—Guy Jensen

Artist's Note

If you have ever stood in Olsen Park and seen the Logan Temple lit up in the crisp chilly air of a Cache Valley Winter, you know that it's a sight indeed. People often describe to me their first dates and proposals that have taken place with this awesome backdrop.

LOGAN'S ELEVATION IS ALMOST 4,800 FEET—PRODUCING SOME VERY COLD WINTERS.

In the heart of Logan lies Central Park whose frozen pond lures skaters out of their warm houses to enjoy an evening of ice skating under the stars and the crescent moon.

Central Park was renamed Merlin Olsen Park to commemorate legendary NFL defensive tackle Merlin Olsen—who happened to grow up in a little, white house across the street from Central Park.

As a youngster, Merlin spent countless hours ice skating at the park. "I loved that park. It was one of the reasons I ended up being a success in football. I ice-skated so much that I developed very powerful legs. I had a hockey puck and a stick—the only ones in town. I definitely would have played hockey ahead of football—had it been available."

The cold weather in Logan is also very conducive to indoor activities. The Ellen Eccles Theatre, built in 1923, is the home of the Utah Festival Opera Company. The theatre—an 1100-seat, European style theatre, was named after Ellen Eccles, wife of Mormon Industrialist, David Eccles.

And of course, during some very cold days in the winter of 1922 (and surrounded by all those cows), it didn't take long for Utah State Professor Gustav Wilster to create Aggie Ice Cream and some revolutionary manufacturing techniques for making ice cream commercially. The Creamery at Utah State became the model for ice creameries all over the country.

LOGAN FALL

Artist's Note

The vibrant colors of Logan in the fall led me to my first oil paining. I had been strongly encouraged to explore the brighter colors of oils and the fiery hews of autumn in Cache Valley seemed to require it. There is the feeling of a New England fall in the air as the aspen trees change colors and give up their leaves.

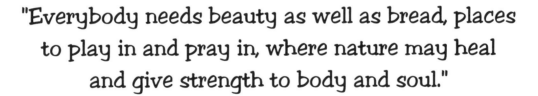

NATURAL WONDERS

"Everybody needs beauty as well as bread, places
to play in and pray in, where nature may heal
and give strength to body and soul."

John Muir

Bear Lake

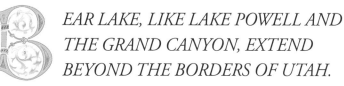

"Keep your eyes open at dusk and maybe you'll see The Bear Lake Monster come out to feed. Just be careful swimming in the lake, or you might be its next meal!"
—S. E. Schlosser

Artist's Note

Bear Lake really is that blue! My family, like many families, loves our time spent there. After spending a day on the lake, then eating a large old Ephraim Pizza with everything on it and trying to finish a large raspberry shake by myself, the inspiration for the painting came naturally.

BEAR LAKE, LIKE LAKE POWELL AND THE GRAND CANYON, EXTEND BEYOND THE BORDERS OF UTAH.

All three are shared with other states. Bear Lake is half in Utah and half in Idaho. However, once you are on the lake, there are no real boundaries. In that moment, Utah belongs to the lake and you are swallowed up by it as well.

Your senses are bathed in the spectacular, bluish hue of this inland sea, or the Caribbean of the Rockies as it has been called. The cool breeze lulls you into a false sense of security while the golden summer sun imperceptibly turns your unprotected skin to the lovely shade of a ripe pomegranate.

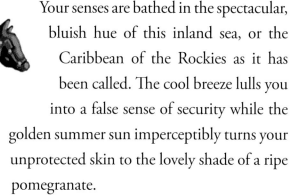

Of course, the original lovers of this lake were the Native American Shoshone Tribes. French-Canadian trappers dropped in for a while in 1818 and, between 1825 and 1840, mountain men such as Jedediah Smith and Jim Bridger met with Native Americans on the south shore to swap goods and stories. Rendezvous Beach to this day is still the location of the annual Mountain Man Rendezvous held in mid-September.

The permanent visitors to Bear Lake, like most places in the challenging environment of the mountain west, were Mormon Pioneers. In this case, the settlers were led by Charles C. Rich, who made several amicable agreements with the Native Americans, which allowed the Saints to set up several permanent towns, including Garden City, Pickleville, and Laketown.

The Bear Lake region is also famous for raspberries. Year after year, the climate and soil of the area produce some of the finest raspberries to be found anywhere. Garden City sponsors an annual Raspberry Days festival during the first week in August. People come from all over the world to attend. The event features rodeos, parades, fireworks, dances, a craft fair, a raspberry recipe cook-off, a talent show, fun run, and concerts. And of course Miss Berry Princess must be chosen. It's all berry fun.

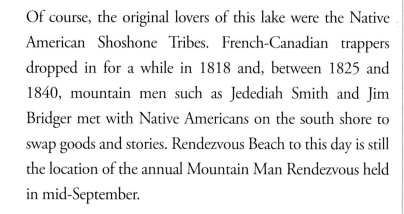

LAKE POWELL

Artist's Note

Lake Powell is where everyone seems to go in Utah when they really want to get away from it all. For me, it is the perfect place to unwind. You can be so alone that even skinny dipping feels safe ...or so I've heard.

DELICATE ARCH

Artist's Note

A book about Utah wouldn't be complete without the Delicate Arch. When I hiked in to see it for the first time, it was a rather warm day in the desert. It was exciting, however, to see how many different people were also making the same journey to see this natural icon. They appeared to be from all over the world.

Lake Powell
Ticaboo, Utah

THE GRAND CANYON

Artist's Note

The Grand Canyon actually begins in Utah, so I felt it had to be in this book. I don't believe any painting could ever do the Grand Canyon complete justice. This painting was laid out to capture some of the stories and important historical figures who helped make the Grand Canyon a must see destination as you travel through southern Utah.

HE ORIGINAL SETTLERS OF UTAH CAME WITH ONLY WHAT THEY COULD CARRY IN SMALL WAGONS AND ON THEIR BACKS.

The settlers came to respect the majesty, power, beauty, and danger of nature. The taming of their surroundings and environment without spoiling it became an important part of Utah's history and heritage. One hundred fifty years later, when we want to relax, we can enjoy what they preserved. We camp, we boat, we hike, and we swim. We climb rocks. We practically invented mountain biking. And that is just in the summer.

The Grand Canyon, although located in Arizona, begins its formation right here in Utah. Carved by the Colorado River, the Grand Canyon is one of Mother Earth's most spectacular natural phenomena, and one of the primary gateways to Grand Canyon National Park is Kanab, Utah. Thousands from Utah make the trek every year to experience the natural beauty of one of our country's greatest landmarks.

Moab has become a very popular destination for rock climbing, mountain biking, and hiking the spectacular trails and rock formations in the area. People come from all over the world to

experience this very unique location.

Moab is considered by many as a true resort town for very discerning travelers who yearn for adventures completely off the main road, or with no road at all.

The Delicate Arch received its current name in 1933. Before then it was called "Chaps" or "School Marm's Bloomers" by the local cowboys. The entrada sandstone was carved over many years of wind, rain, and freezing winter temperatures, into the amazing image that is now an icon for the state. There are many pictures of the Delicate Arch but nothing quite beats the actual sculpture.

Lake Powell is houseboat heaven. Houseboats abound over this man-made lake that is 400 feet deep, 186 miles long, with 2000 miles of shoreline. A houseboat vacation at Lake Powell is unique because one may have all of the comforts of home in the middle of nowhere. There are no dwellings in sight or any other hints of civilization. Just you, 20 other people, a boat, a few jet skis, enough food and drink for a month (that you will eat in a week), and you have the perfect vacation.

ALONG THE WAY

"Travel is more than the seeing of sights; it is a change that
goes on, deep and permanent, in the ideas of living."

Miriam Beard

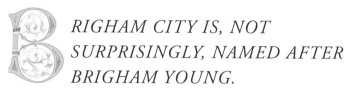

Artist's Note

While living in Idaho, my family would often drive to Utah to visit relatives and go to Lagoon. Before the freeway was completed, the only road leading to Salt Lake City was Highway 89 and it went right through Brigham City. My memory of Brigham City was one great big fruit stand that stretched from one end of the city to the other. On one trip the family van broke down in Brigham City. We happily ate bushels of fresh fruit while repairs were being made. We were never so thrilled to be stranded.

BRIGHAM CITY

BRIGHAM CITY IS, NOT SURPRISINGLY, NAMED AFTER BRIGHAM YOUNG.

It had been known as Box Elder for over 22 years. The name change was a loving tribute to Brother Brigham, after he gave one of his last public sermons here in 1877.

Brigham City was designed, from its founding, as a completely self-sufficient city. In 1853 Brigham Young called Lorenzo Snow to build a city founded on the principles of cooperative living. Brother Snow recruited people by trade to move to the new city.

Carpenters, blacksmiths, farmers, administrators, and school teachers were among those whom Lorenzo called to join him in this attempt to live these principles of self reliance. It actually worked well for the first two and half decades, but financial difficulties in the state eventually took its toll on the community and important assets were sold to compensate. The venture came to a close at the end of the century, but a strong, tight-knit community remained.

World War II brought economic prosperity to the area when the federal government built Bushnell General Hospital on Brigham City's south side to treat soldiers injured in the war. Farms and orchards prospered as food and supplies were needed for the massive medical facility. Government employees, doctors, and nurses patronized the local businesses. Despite the war, times were good in Brigham City.

To this day Brigham City continues to attract industry. Many companies that are happy to locate here to take advantage of the highly educated workforce. Thiokol builds solid rocket motors for the space shuttle and Autoliv has a large factory that builds air bags for automobiles. It is still the busy community Brigham Young envisioned.

As Brigham City's *Past and Future* travel sticker above suggests, this oasis on the interstate has gone from the horse and buggy into outer space. But when you visit this busy little town and stop at a local fruit stand you will see that Brigham City hasn't lost one bit of its charm.

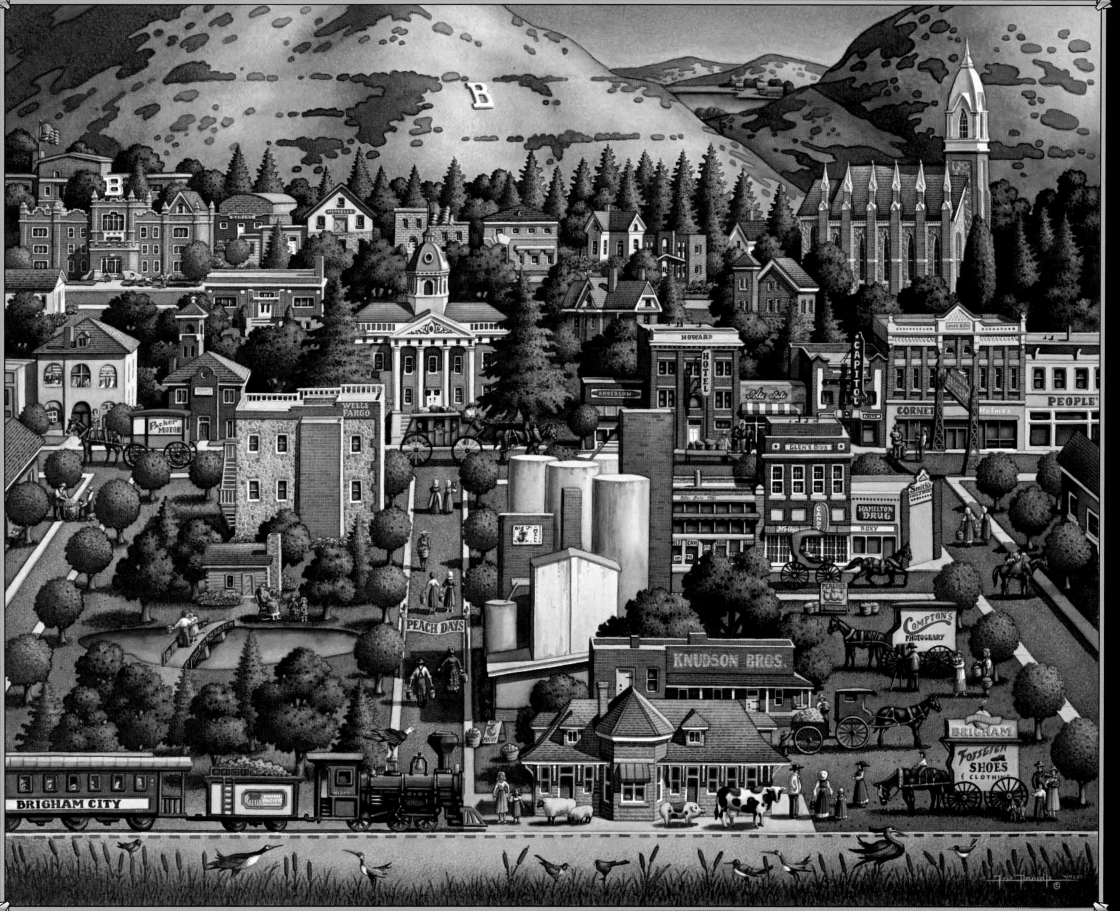

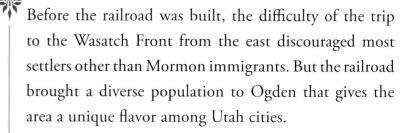

OGDEN

GDEN IS UTAH'S RAILROAD TOWN! IT OPERATED BOTH A NORTH-SOUTH AND EAST-WEST HUB.

It soon became known as the *Crossroads of the West.* Many even called it *Junction City.*

The Golden Spike, which joined the Central Pacific and Union Pacific Railroads, is not far from Ogden. It was an event that helped shape the entire country, and Ogden was privileged to be a big part of the growth of the nation's rail system.

Originally, Ogden was a typical western settlement. Founded by trappers from the Hudson Bay Company, the city derived its name in honor of Peter Skein Ogden, one of those first trappers.

Before the railroad was built, the difficulty of the trip to the Wasatch Front from the east discouraged most settlers other than Mormon immigrants. But the railroad brought a diverse population to Ogden that gives the area a unique flavor among Utah cities.

The railroad transformed Ogden into a major industrial center. Livestock yards, flour mills, iron works, woolen mills, telephone, telegraph, and power companies all sprung up here and thrived. Investment capital from back east saw many opportunities here. Banks, hotels, and multiple government installations continue to employ thousands to this very day. Hill Air Force Base, the Army Defense Depot, and the Clearfield Navel Supply Center add a mighty boost to the local economy.

Ogden today is alive with sound. From the constant rumble of shunting trains and speeding cars, to the buzzing of jet fighters overhead, Ogden may be more than just a crossroad of travel. It may also be a crossroad of time; between the past, the present, and the future.

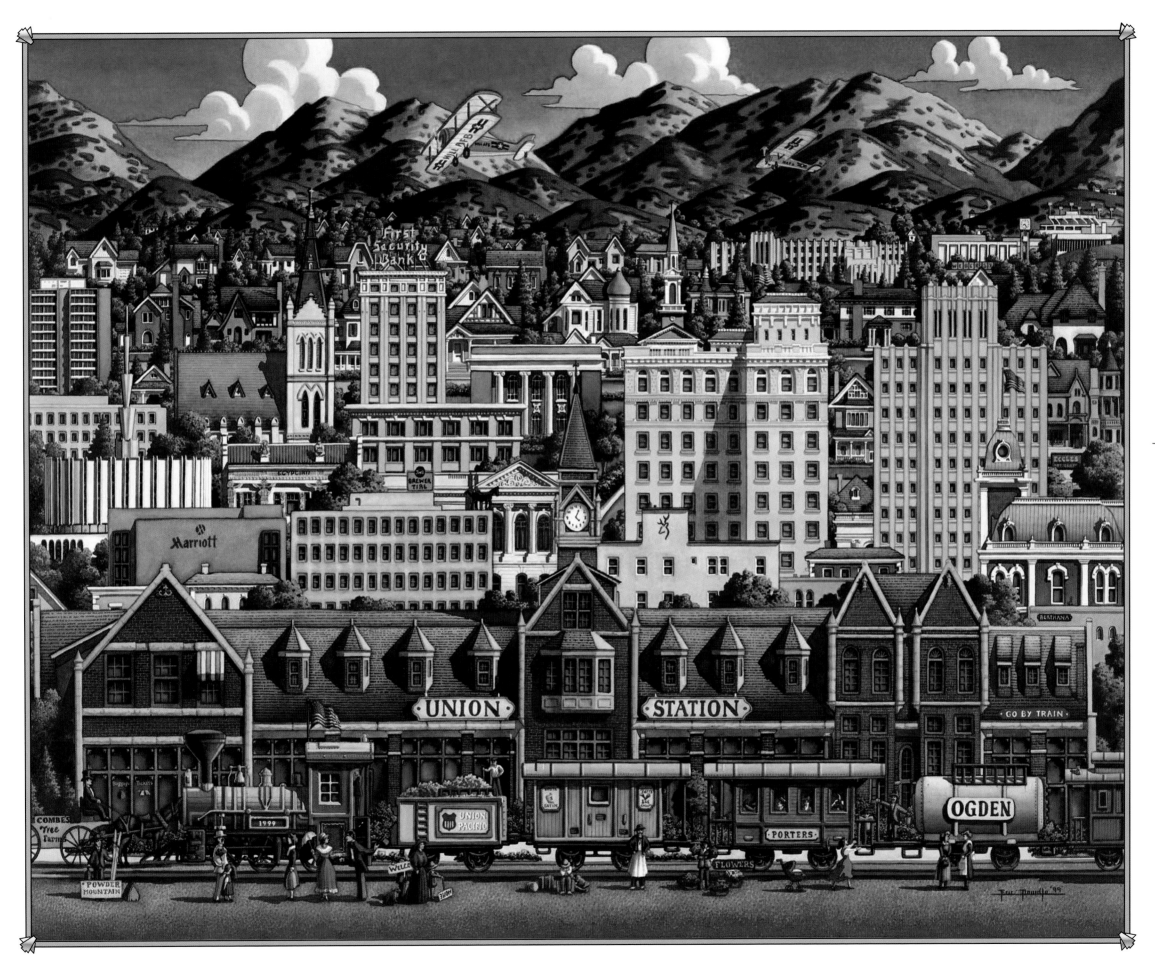

Artist's Note

Everybody cut footloose! Before starting this painting, I toured Lehi Roller Mills and learned more about flour and Kevin Bacon than I ever thought I would need. The mill grinds some of the best flour in the world and is a beloved icon for Utah.

LEHI ROLLER MILLS

EHI, LIKE BRIGHAM CITY AND OGDEN, IS LOCATED JUST A FEW FEET FROM THE INTERSTATE. JUST EXIT THE FREEWAY AND IN LESS THAN A MINUTE, YOU ARE IN DOWNTOWN LEHI.

The skyscrapers of Lehi aren't office towers or apartment buildings like some cities. They are grain elevators. Lehi Roller Mills is one of the most recognizable structures in Utah. Still a fully functional mill, it grinds flour around the clock, six days a week. It produces nearly 100,000 pounds of flour each day.

Lehi, (named for a Book of Mormon prophet) is a farming community nestled near the head of Utah Lake between the Salt Lake Valley and Provo. Each farm was originally a 40-acre plot portioned out to individual settlers.

Lehi Roller Mills was founded in 1906 by a co-op of farmers. It was purchased by George G. Robinson soon after that and has remained in his family ever since. It is one of less than 50 remaining family-owned mills in the United States. Once there were thousands.

Lehi, was immortalized in the 1984 movie, Footloose, starring Kevin Bacon, Lori Singer, John Lithgow, Dianne Wiest, and the Lehi Roller Mills. The mill was the location of Kevin Bacon's famous dance sequence in the movie. The recognition that Lehi Roller Mills received from that movie has made the mill a Utah icon forever.

The city of Lehi even celebrates this fact by holding a "Footloose" dance every July 13 right off Main Street. Unlike the movie, dancing is actually encouraged in Lehi.

U
T
A
H

CHILDHOOD DAYS

"I'd give all wealth that years have piled,
The slow result of Life's decay,
To be once more a little child
For one bright summer day."

Lewis Carroll, *Solitude*

HIDE AND SEEK

Artist's Note

One of the great things about living in Utah is that there are plenty of children. It took only a few phone calls to round up enough kids for the Hide-n-Seek painting. My friends from Sugarhouse and their children get credit for this favorite childhood scene. This whimsical house can be found on Main Street in Midway. It is a classic John Watkins designed home.

UTAH AND LARGE HAPPY FAMILIES HAVE ALMOST BECOME A STEREOTYPE, IF NOT A CLICHÉ.

The Latter Day Saint pioneers came to the Salt Lake Valley, cleared the fields, planted crops, and began raising large families to help with the monumental task of taming the land and building communities suitable for family life. In those early days of Utah, children were seen as blessings who, when not in school, would work the land right next to the adults.

However, Brigham Young taught that all work and no play was not the Utah way. Each community had an entertainment hall and many civic activities were planned to entice families away from the farm to enjoy fun and games. At home, dad was often the taskmaster, but mom would often step up as the one in charge of fun and recreation, once the chores were done.

The love of family and family togetherness was taught from the pulpit and the soapbox. Children were taught to love and respect their elders, love their country, and live moral, value-centered lives. Families worked together, played together, and on Sundays, they went to church together. *Family values* were not a political issue; they were practically the only issue. Today, in an effort to maintain this important cultural tradition, many Utahans dedicate one evening a week as *Family Night*, where the whole family puts everything aside to spend a few uninterrupted hours together.

Today Utah families are just slightly larger than the national average by 1/2 child per family. Also, Utah families, like the rest of the U.S. populace, come in all shapes, colors and sizes. And, whatever their family makeup, most agree, Utah is a pretty great state in which to raise a family.

SCHOOL CARNIVAL

THE SAINTS ARRIVED IN THE SALT LAKE VALLEY IN 1847. THAT SAME YEAR MARY JANE DILWORTH STARTED THE FIRST SCHOOL IN UTAH.

Education and schools have been important to Utah since the beginning. The Mormon pioneers were a well-educated group as a whole and consequently they put a high priority on education for their children. Utah's first schools were typical frontier cooperative efforts that involved parents and communities banding together to support each school.

Brigham Young began, almost immediately, sending select saints back east on *educational missions* to become proficient in various disciplines and then return to Utah to teach the next generation of teachers the latest information on each subject.

This noble heritage is the foundation for Utah schools today. Utah has 936 schools, 818 public and 118 private, consisting of 555 elementary schools, 126 middle schools, and 180 high schools—and what a task these

schools perform. Fifteen percent of Utah's population is elementary school age children—the highest percentage in the United States. It is no wonder that schools play such a central role in the lives of Utah families. The bake sale, car wash, or carnival brings whole communities together to support local school activities. Everyone plays a part.

Utah schools are hubs of activity and entertainment. They are filled with science projects and historic discoveries. They provide a seemingly endless cavalcade of musical concerts, theatrical productions, and sporting events. They are the social centers for Utah children from kindergarten through high school.

The successful partnership between schools and parents that began with the pioneers still exists in the Utah educational system. Utah schools test way above the national average. The goal is to give children the knowledge and character they need to graduate beyond Utah's borders, if they choose, and experience the world and beyond.

Artist's Note

As a tribute to the Utah PTA for their contribution to our children, I painted a nostalgic fund-raising carnival. The St. George Woodward School was used as a backdrop, making my favorite people and activities come alive. I've depicted my wife and myself as children in the painting. My wife is holding her favorite flower and I'm holding a pet chicken from my childhood.

CAMP EAGLES NEST

THE BOY SCOUTS OF AMERICA WAS INCORPORATED ON FEBRUARY 8, 1910 AND UTAHNS ADOPTED THE PROGRAM SOON AFTER.

It was part of the larger world scouting organization founded by Robert Baden-Powell to improve the character of young men.

Utah's heritage seemed to be a perfect match for the ideals of this new organization. The first scout troop in Utah was formed in Centerville in 1912, just two years after the BSA's formation. Since that time the scouting program has flourished in Utah. School and church groups throughout the state sponsor Boy Scout troops making this opportunity available to every young man in the state who wishes to participate. Sixty percent of scouting age boys in Utah belong to the Boy Scouts of America, compared to nineteen percent for the national average.

Utah has 28 sanctioned Boy Scout camps. Every summer these camps are alive with activity. Boys from all

over the state come to these adolescent retreats to learn about life, the great outdoors, and about their own abilities to deal with innumerable challenges placed before them. Earning merit badges is one of the goals at Boy Scout camps. It is possible for a young man to earn over 120 different types of merit badges covering everything from camping and hiking to nuclear science.

Leadership training is also a very important part of scouting. As a scout achieves different ranks they are required to assume various leadership responsibilities. Ranks include, Tenderfoot, Second Class, First Class, Star, Life, and Eagle Scouts. Each rank requires various merit badge and leadership achievements. The rank of Eagle Scout is considered an accomplishment that will help any young man achieve success for the rest of his life. Utah produces three times the national average of Eagle Scouts for those who participate in the program.

Artist's Note

Scouting is as entrenched in the Utah culture as Jell-O and seagulls. Utah produces more eagle scouts than any other state. It's part of our culture. Camp Eagle's Nest is a tribute to my parent's commitment to the principles taught in scouting. The ten nests in the painting represent each child in my family that earned their Eagle. Ten boys ... ten eagles. I had a lot of fun capturing all the fun and work from a scout camp experience. My inspiration comes from Camp Maple Dell, just outside of Payson.

U
T
A
H

RESORT LIVING

"Skiing combines outdoor fun with knocking
down trees with your face."

Dave Barry

PARK CITY

Artist's Note

One day I met a lady at my gallery who had just moved to Spanish Fork from "New Joyzee". She looked a little lost and out of place. I asked her how the transition was going. Her response told me that she needed to discover Park City. I sent her on her way, knowing she would have a great experience. Much has changed in Park City since this painting was completed, but it still remains one of my family's great escapes.

EADING EAST FROM SALT LAKE CITY INVOLVES A 3,000 FOOT CLIMB IN ELEVATION TO PARK CITY.

Park City was, surprisingly, listed in the mid-twentieth century as one of the great ghost towns of the west! Now it is one of the wealthiest cities in the United States. "There's gold in them thar hills!" is an aphorism that paid off twice for Park City: first, as a mining town and then, nearly one hundred years later, as a major ski resort town. Between times of prosperity, however, there were some difficult years for Park City.

In October 1868, some soldiers climbed over the mountains from Big Cottonwood Canyon to the Park City area and found traces of silver. Because snow was swirling and a storm brewing, they marked their claim with a bandanna on a stick and returned the following spring.

By 1870, Parley's Park City—as it was first named after the early settler Parley Pratt, and then shortened to just Park City—had a total population of 164. After the discovery of gold, lead, and silver in the area, Park City became so populated it was thought it could replace Salt Lake City as the primary city of Utah.

Park City was one of the few Utah cities established by non-

Mormons. At one time it had 27 saloons ligning Main Street, even during Prohibition. The bet was that no one could take a drink at each establishment in a single night and remain standing.

Park City was the third city in Utah to boast having telephone service and the first to have electricity. By statehood day, January 5, 1896, there were more than 7,000 residents, and by the turn of the century over 10,000 populated the city!

Before the mining industry collapsed in the area, over $400 million was taken from the mountains. More than 23 millionaires were created, including George Hearst, William Randolph Hearst's father. For nearly a half century after the ore gave out, Park City didn't really know what to do with itself. It languished into an old western town of forgotten dreams…

SKI PARK CITY

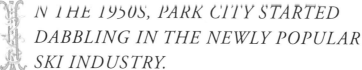

IN THE 1950S, PARK CITY STARTED DABBLING IN THE NEWLY POPULAR SKI INDUSTRY.

Before that time, during the winter, several miners transported themselves around the mountains using 'long board snowshoes'— a predecessor to skis. In 1906, a telephone company lineman used skis to help him troubleshoot the lines between Alta, Brighton, and Park City. It was these early experiments with skiing that were to save the town from oblivion over the next several years.

In 1963, Park City qualified for a federal loan from the Area Redevelopment Agency and developed the Treasure Mountain Resort— Park City Mountain Resort, today. A gondola, a chair lift, and two J-bars were installed. A lift pass cost $3.50 and there were 50,000 skier days logged that first year. As word of the new ski area spread, people started to flock to Park City. The old machinery of the mining industry now protrudes from the mountains as icons of days gone by, while skiers from all over the world whiz by on some of the most expensive real estate in the country. More than 40 percent of the events of the 2002 Winter Olympic Games were held at various Park City ski and winter resorts.

Park City boasts as its residents some of the most recognizable names in entertainment and business; and why not? Year round, it is a great place to live and play. The allure of Park City's Main Street combines the nostalgia of the past with some of the most elegant restaurants and eclectic shops around. It is the ultimate outdoor mall!

Park City is also home to the Sundance Film Festival, the largest independent film festival in the United States. Robert Redford, who fell in love with Utah's natural beauty while making a movie here, created this world-renowned competition. The rich and famous crowd onto Main Street and mingle with anybody fortunate enough to buy a ticket for one of the many films shown at this spectacular event.

Park City's future continues to look very bright. The city is aggressively preserving the past while planning for years of prosperity ahead. Park City may have had most of the precious ore removed from its hills, but the city itself stands as a jewel in the mountains of Utah.

PARK CITY
PARK CITY
BREEZE
KI RENTAL
MAX
SNOWBOARD
Rocky Mountain
CHOCOLATE FACTORY
Eric Dowdle©

SNOWED INN

*T*HE CONCEPT OF THE COUNTRY INN IS AS OLD AS TIME; HOWEVER, THE TERM 'BED AND BREAKFAST' COMES FROM THE BRITISH ISLES.

Perhaps it is that heritage that makes the Utah Bed and Breakfast experience so popular. Many Utahns leave their own warm homes and drive 20 minutes up the canyon just to stay in the snug, old-world environment of a bed and breakfast. They are popular year round, but seem to be even more inviting and special on cold, wintry evenings. Of course, it may also be the homemade pancakes, muffins, and fruit served the next morning that makes traveling to one of the many *B&Bs* in the state one of Utah's favorite getaways.

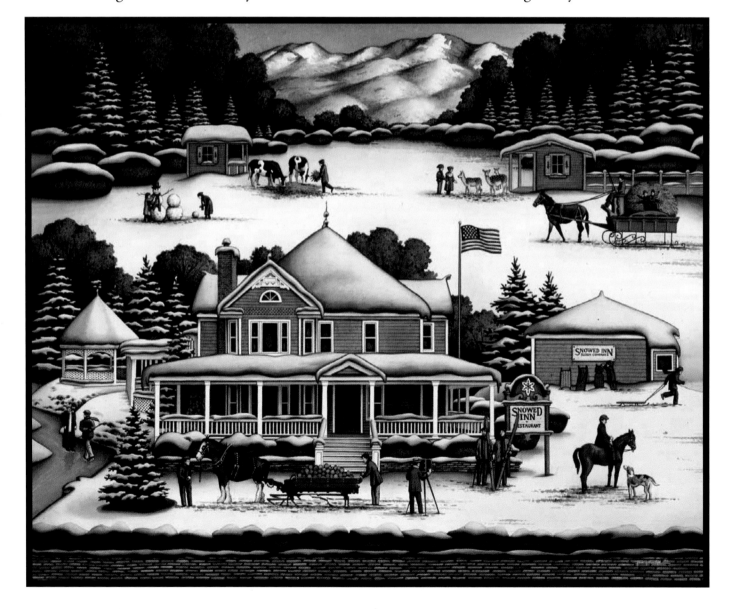

Artist's Note

Deep in the wintry hills of Park City I discovered a scene that belongs in a Christmas snow-globe. The Snowed Inn was once a charming bed and breakfast that my wife and I visited a number of times. It's now a private school, but back then it offered a winter wonderland experience that captured the imagination.

Inn for the Evening

Artist's Note

Inspired by my "Snowed Inn" painting and the beautiful architecture of Midway, this painting was to have been part of a Utah "Inn" series. The series never materialized but this old Utah landmark remains a good representation of the many charming Utah inns and Bed and Breakfasts that await the weary traveler.

A Taste of The Alps

"Doubly happy, however, is the man to whom
lofty mountain-tops are within reach."

John Muir

Heber

THE FIRST WHITE MEN TO PASS THROUGH BEAUTIFUL HEBER VALLEY WERE SPANISH FRIARS looking for a passageway between Santa Fe, New Mexico, and Monterrey, California. For the following hundred years, only hunters and trappers in search of beaver and mink visited the area—often using trails and footpaths created by Indians.

Early settlers in the area were Mormon converts from England—many of whom had been introduced to The Church of Jesus Christ of Latter-day Saints by Heber C. Kimball. They decided to name the valley and the first settlement after him. The first harvest in the valley was in 1859, but residents returned to Salt Lake City until the following spring when they could build dwellings fit for the cold winter days of a high mountain valley.

The Heber City area has depended for years on agriculture, livestock, and dairy farming as its main industry. Once the Rio Grande Western railway track was completed in 1899, the city became the shipping center for agricultural products. By 1915, the railroad was boasting that Heber was shipping 360 cars of sheep, 280 cars of hay, 40 cars of cattle, and 60 cars of sugar beets each year. During the 1930's, more sheep were shipped from the Heber depot than from any other rail station in the nation.

Soon after the railroad was established to carry freight between Heber City and Provo, a passenger car was added on the rear of the train. The mixed cargo train generally crept along the curving canyon track at a slow rate of speed—earning the train the nickname *Creeper*. The *Heber Creeper* was so slow that, according to one story, a newlywed couple boarded the train in Provo and had their first child as the train pulled into the Heber station.

In 1887, volunteer laborers began construction on the Heber City Tabernacle. Red sandstone was quarried by hand from the mountains east of Heber and shingles for the tower were cut from sheet metal. The tabernacle was dedicated in May 1889. In 1987, the city voted to restore the tabernacle for use as a city hall. It stands proudly in the center of town as a reminder of those early pioneers.

MIDWAY

MIDWAY GOT ITS NAME ORIGINALLY BECAUSE IT WAS HALFWAY BETWEEN TWO OTHER SETTLEMENTS.

Today, Midway, a verdant high-mountain valley, feels like it's halfway to heaven.

In the 1860s and 1870s a large number of Swiss immigrants moved into the area. Those that settled here and then stayed for generations include the Gertsch, Huber, Kohler, Probst, Zenger, Durtschi, and Abegglen families, among others. The unusual thing wasn't that these people were from Switzerland, it was more that they brought Switzerland with them.

More than the average Utah settlement, Midway has held onto its old-world heritage with a tenacity that almost makes Midway residents capable of applying for dual citizenship. The beauty and order of a small Swiss town has existed in Midway now for generations

and everybody wants to keep it that way. For example, ordinances have been passed that require buildings to have a Swiss influence in their design.

Many activities and celebrations have a Swiss theme, culminating on Labor-ay weekend every year when the Swiss Days Festival is held. People come from all over to participate in one of the largest outdoor boutiques in the entire West. The origin of Swiss Days dates back to the late 1940's as a harvest celebration. It was named Swiss Days so that the townsfolk could dress in their traditional Swiss attire and celebrate old world customs. The festival raises large amounts of money for civic projects and activities.

Midway, has a small population of a little over 2000 people, but that doesn't include the thousands of people who are visiting year round in the several resorts operating in the town. Midway resorts have become a destination for Utahns to come and enjoy family activities and togetherness in the splendor of the Alp-like mountains surrounding the area. Just a short 40-minute drive from Salt Lake City and you feel like you are in Switzerland. And the amenities and atmosphere hint that you have not only traveled to a different country, you have arrived into another time!

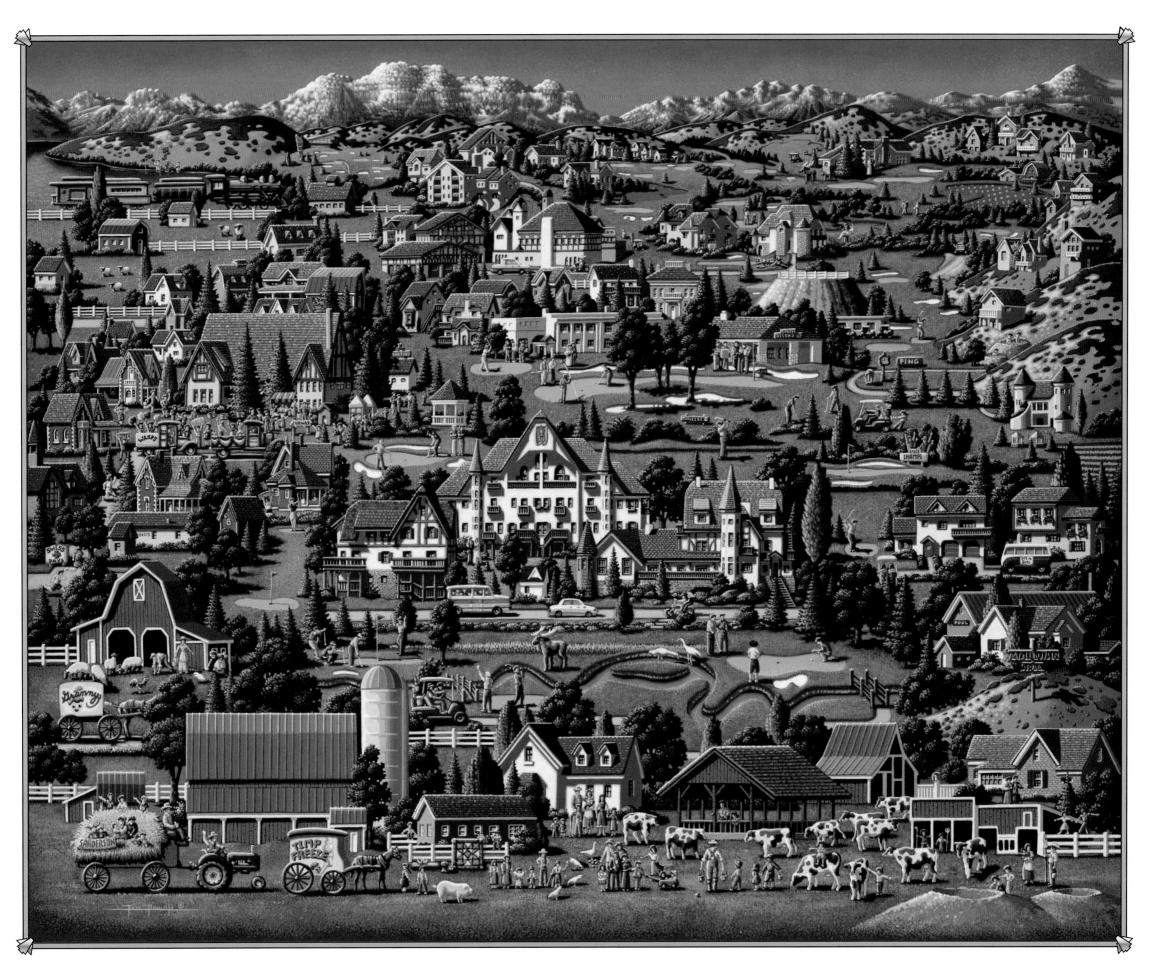

GINGERBREAD HOUSE

EVERY ONCE IN A WHILE AS YOU TRAVEL THROUGHOUT THIS GREAT STATE YOU COME ACROSS A SITE THAT SEEMS, WELL, MAGICAL.

It almost appears as though what you are staring at belongs in a storybook rather than the framing crops of your camera. Such is the case with several of the whimsical homes in Midway, Utah.

Designed by local Utah architects, these homes, technically, were designed in the Gothic Revival style, but they look like they could be made out of gingerbread and frosting. As you stare, you can imagine a master pastry chef inside baking a batch of cookies. Pause long enough and you can almost smell them. Pause even longer and you start imagining the cookies escaping from the oven and racing around the twilight neighborhood.

Not everyone that sees this idyllic scene imagines such an event but the sight of these homes does excite the imagination. While exploring Utah, take a leisurely drive up Provo Canyon, sneak past Heber, and coast into Midway and you will see for yourself.

Artist's Note

Inspired by the Swiss architecture of Midway, I created my own Christmas village covered with gingerbread cookies. Each cookie depicts a celebrity or icon in American culture. Entertainers, historical figures, sports stars, and yes... some notorious characters are represented. Have fun as a family trying to figure out who each cookie represents.

U
T
A
H

OFF THE BEATEN PATH

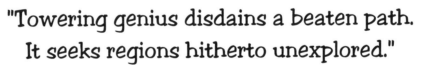

"Towering genius disdains a beaten path.
It seeks regions hitherto unexplored."

Abraham Lincoln

ALPINE SUMMER

Artist's Note

Of all my art releases, Alpine Summer was one of my favorites. We invited the entire town to the park for an Americana Picnic. We served pie, played band music and partied for hours at the well-known white gazebo. Families came, shared stories, laughed and played hard. The people of Alpine truly love their town.

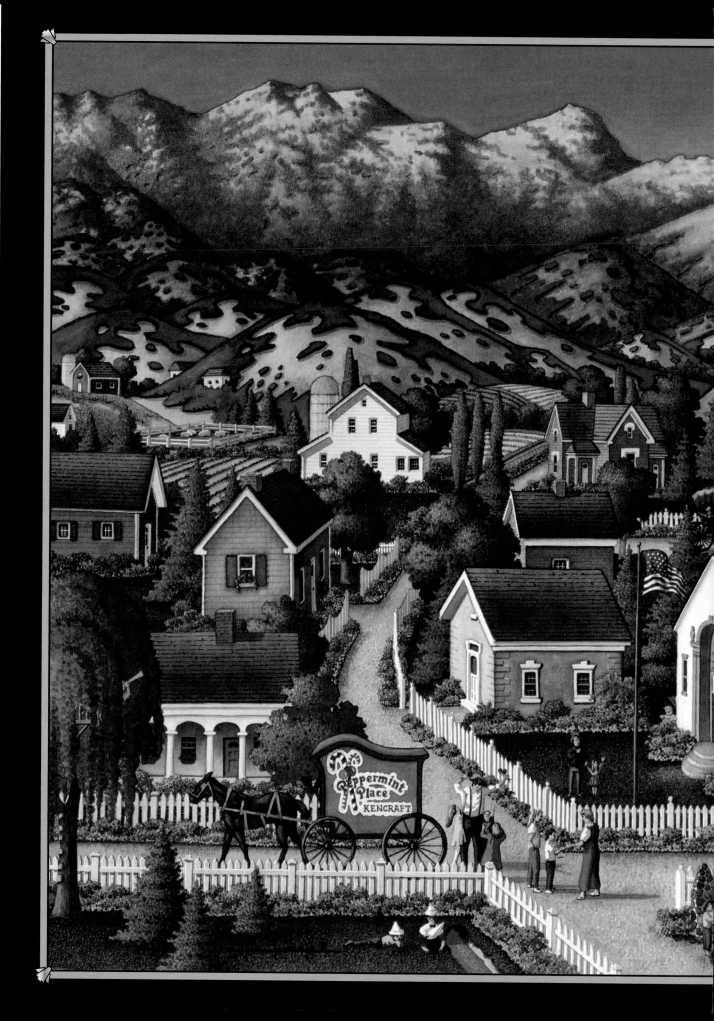

MANTI & ALPINE

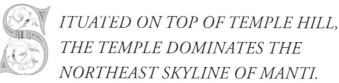

SITUATED ON TOP OF TEMPLE HILL, THE TEMPLE DOMINATES THE NORTHEAST SKYLINE OF MANTI.

Brigham Young announced the construction of the temple in June, 1875, and it was completed in 1888. Before the announcement, Temple Hill was known as the Manti Stone Quarry. To survive the severe winter of 1849, Manti's first settlers had to live in temporary shelters dug into the hill.

Manti is the home of the Mormon Miracle Pageant, an annual outdoor theatrical performance produced with an amateur cast of over five hundred. The nightly program takes place in June on the south lawn of Temple Hill.

This production has the largest attendance of any outdoor pageant in the U.S., attracting an average of 100,000 visitors every year. The average nightly attendance hovers around 15,000. Since 1967, more than 4.2 million visitors have come to view this annual event.

Manti has preserved more than 100 buildings that were built by pioneer craftsmen—more than any other city in Utah. Many of these buildings predate the civil war. Most of the structures are built of *oolite* limestone quarried from the hills behind the temple and are easily seen if you take the Historic Manti City Walking Tour. You have to go out of your way to get to Manti, however, just like Alpine it is a destination all its own.

In the far northeast corner of Utah Valley, near the mouth of American Fork Canyon, lies the quiet, almost hidden, community of Alpine. Settled in 1850 by cattle ranchers, Alpine was known by a host of names including Fort Wordsworth, Upper Dry Creek Settlement, Lone City, and Mountainville—because of the bordering high mountains. Territorial Governor Brigham Young was reported to have liked the name Mountainville, but considered Alpine more appropriate. In January 1855, the Mountainville settlement was officially incorporated as the City of Alpine. It is considered one of the nicest bedroom communities along the Wasatch front.

Alpine features the Peppermint Place in its city center—a confectionery wonderland offering a free behind-the-scenes look at the candy-crafting process in all of its sticky splendor. Children from all over drag their parents to visit this Willy Wonka-like paradise that features a 90,000-square-foot factory and store specializing in a countless variety of goodies.

ALPINE CHRISTMAS

Artist's Note

I sat and discussed with the Alpine "old-timers" stories of the cold winters of yesteryear. One sweet white-haired woman rehearsed to me how her family would hitch up the sleigh and horses in November and wouldn't un-hitch until March. We all chuckled as each person matched stories and reminisced about precious days gone by.

MANTI

Artist's Note

As I painted Manti from my Cottonwood Mall gallery, the woman who would later become my wife strolled by. As we chatted I painted her name in the grass. Little did I know that one day she would be forever mine. Speaking of life-long loves, take some time to find the cows sporting their preferred college or Universities. I enjoy in-state sport rivalries.

U
T
A
H

HAPPY VALLEY

Root ⁊

" Beer is living proof that God loves us and wants us to be happy."

Benjamin Franklin

PROVO

"Provo is one of the soberest cities in the United States. The fact that they call this place 'Happy Valley' may just mean that Provo knows something that the rest of us don't."
—Anonymous Visitor

Artist's Note

As an eight-year-old boy living on a farm in Boise, Idaho, I dreamed of one day moving to the enchanting city of Provo. That was when I started following the Brigham Young Cougars religiously. In my mind I imagined the people of Provo to all be ultra nice and super cool. Thirty years later I live a stones-throw away from my dream and have found my imaginings to be quite accurate.

UTAH VALLEY WAS THE TRADITIONAL HOME OF THE UTE INDIANS. THEY STAYED CLOSE TO UTAH LAKE AS IT CONTAINED ONE OF THEIR MAIN SOURCES OF FOOD—FISH.

When first settled in 1849 by 33 Mormon families from Salt Lake City, Provo was called Fort Utah. It was later renamed Provo for Etienne Provost, a French-Canadian trapper who is thought to be the first person of European descent to see the Great Salt Lake.

In 1858, most Salt Lake City residents, including Brigham Young, temporarily moved to Provo in response to President James Buchanan's *Mormon War*. After the saints were "pardoned," Provo remained Utah's second largest city until the railroad made Ogden a main stop on the transcontinental railroad.

Provo proved to have ideal soil and climate for fruit trees and gardens and soon came to be known as the Garden City. Many of the orchards still exist today, but each year several are replaced by modern developments and beautiful homes.

Provo has, since its founding, been a center of commerce and development in Utah County. In the late 19th century, agriculture and the Utah Woolen Mills thrived. In the 20th century, Provo joined the industrial revolution with the advent of a successful steel mill and other industries derived from successful mining ventures. At the latter part of the century, Provo became a miniature *Silicone Valley* with companies such as Word Perfect and Novell leading the way.

Today, Provo is considered the most conservative city in America; nearly ninety percent of Utah Valley residents are members of the Church of Jesus Christ of Latter-day Saints. In the last 15 years, the Provo-Orem community has regularly been named in the top ten places to live in America. People living here have felt that way for over 150 years.

USA
Dunford
RWH
EDWARDS
Stadium of Fire
BYU
TRAUMA AWARENESS CENTER
AMERICA'S FREEDOM FESTIVAL at PROVO.
Smith Auto
I LOVE PROVO
Novell
GOD BLESS AMERICA
DC TUXEDOS
Provo
KNEADERS
bakery cafe
ROOT BEER
Eric Dowdle '01

BRIGHAM ACADEMY

In 1895, the Brigham Young Academy and the University of Utah met for the first sporting event between the two schools: a baseball game. The scoreless match ended with a bench-clearing brawl, and a rivalry was born.

—Deseret Morning News, 26 May 2004.

Artist's Note

I guess what I like the most about this piece it that it reminds me of the late Rex Lee, former President of Brigham Young University. The man who purchased the painting donated it to the Lee family months before Rex passed away. The painting shows the humble beginnings of BYU, the institution to which Rex Lee gave so much of his life.

BRIGHAM YOUNG IS THE FATHER OF THE BIGGEST RIVALRY IN THE STATE OF UTAH.

He had part in the founding of two universities: one in Salt Lake City, which became the University of Utah and the second in Provo, which became Brigham Young University.

Like two warring sons of a king, these two schools come together several times a year in athletic competition to fight for state dominance. Football and basketball are particularly heated. There exists a highly volatile mixture of emotions from friendly rivalry to downright disdain between the two respected institutions of higher learning.

The University of Utah was the firstborn of the two, founded in 1850–Brigham Young Academy followed in 1875. For decades the elder school dominated, but then BYU came into its own and, as a result, some of the greatest games in history have been played.

Brigham Young Academy later became Brigham Young University, a leader in technology, law, and other academic pursuits. It is consistently ranked as one of the top private universities in the country. It is also ranked number one on the list of most sober colleges in the United States.

The University of Utah boasts one of the best medical schools around as well as a first-rate law school and business program. It prides itself as being an institution that will allow, on occasion, a celebratory drink or two.

Both schools have brought great honor to Utah. Both schools have produced impressive leaders for the community, state, and country. J. Willard Marriott, the hotel magnate, has contributed to both institutions: the Marriott Library at the University of Utah and the Marriott Center at BYU that was at one time the largest college basketball facility in the U.S.

BYU has remained a private institution, owned by the Church of Jesus Christ of Latter-day Saints, while the University of Utah is a state-owned school. And the rivalry continues...

STORYTELLERS QUILT

THE STORYTELLERS QUILT IS IMPORTANT TO UTAH HISTORY IN AT LEAST TWO WAYS.

First, storytellers around the campfires, as the pioneers headed to Utah, were sometimes the only entertainment for weary travelers after a long day's journey. And, whether it was a story of King Arthur or King David, if the story inspired them to rise and conquer another day, the storyteller succeeded.

Second, in a culture based on teaching and inspiring the world and future generations, storytelling is the fundamental language of all meaningful instruction. From the fables of Aesop to the parables of Christ, stories have been the primary teaching tool of the masters. The Storytellers Quilt is a tribute to these teachers.

Commissioned by Alan and Karen Ashton for the Timpanogos Storytellers' Festival located in Provo, Utah, The Storytellers Quilt shows representations of stories from the greatest storytellers of all time. Their words are carried through the air by a spiral of flying books.

A tapestry of many favorite characters from the greatest stories surround this central image and the whole work is wrapped up in a warm quilt.

The phrase "Happily Ever After," depicted in the painting is part of the daily lexicon in Happy Valley, Utah. More that just a tired phrase here; it describes a way of life, filled with the hope of happiness today and many tomorrows to come.

> "You'll find white tents with their flaps thrown wide and a rapt audience held in the grip of a storyteller's undulating voice. Pass by any tent, listen carefully, and you'll be eavesdropping on the creation of a universe set into motion by the spoken word."
>
> —Jason Smith,
> Salt Lake Magazine

Artist's Note

I love a story as much as anybody and my paintings are filled with them. So when I was asked to do a painting for the Storytellers' Festival I wanted to do something special. The Storytellers Quilt is painted on a 3-dimensional woodcarving. Just like a good story, I wanted the characters to seem like they could jump right out of the image.

U

T

A

H

Fun and Thanksgiving

"For flowers that bloom about our feet;
For tender grass, so fresh, so sweet;
For song of bird, and hum of bee;
For all things fair we hear or see,
Father in heaven, we thank Thee!"

Ralph Waldo Emerson

THANKSGIVING POINT

WHEN THE SAINTS FIRST LOOKED OVER THE SALT LAKE VALLEY, THERE WAS NOTHING BUT TALL BRUSH AND GRASS.

Everything that is in the valley today, a modern metropolis surrounded by factories, housing developments, and rich farmland, is the result of their vision and hard work. Those of us who are beneficiaries of their sacrifice should feel a debt of gratitude—of thanksgiving.

Thanksgiving Point was founded in 1996 by Alan and Karen Ashton on the former site of the Fox Family Farm in Lehi, Utah. Alan Ashton was a co-founder of the software company *WordPerfect* established in Provo, Utah in 1979. The financial success of WordPerfect allowed the Ashtons to fulfill a desire to give something back to the community.

Thanksgiving Point's official web site gives a fascinating insight on the origins of Thanksgiving Point and the inspiration that motivated its creation.

"We wanted to create something for the people around us," says Alan Ashton. "We had been blessed financially and with a large family. We wanted to give something back to the community and the families in our area. Our vision for engaging educational activities was constantly expanding...

Each time we got an idea there were additional things that complemented that idea, so it has grown."

Thanksgiving Point covers several hundred acres now and over the years new sections have been added. Main sites today include Thanksgiving Point Gardens, Golf Course, Life, Farm main building

Thanksgiving Point Museum of Ancient Country, and the complex which contains multiple dining and retail establishments. Each of these venues were planned and created by masters of their crafts. Once you catch your breath it is easy to feel grateful here.

Each year more and more events are being scheduled at Thanksgiving Point. Nearly 1.4 million people visit each year. It has truly become a year-round family destination.

Artist's Note

Thanksgiving Point has been, for several years, a place I have called home showcasing two of my galleries as well as a place for partnering with dear friends in philanthropic ventures. Each year this inviting location becomes more and more a meeting place focused on families in the spirit of gratitude. We love the vision of this place and particularly love the gardens.

ELECTRIC PARK

Artist's Note

Electric Park is known for its fun activities and parties. I am not a big fan of wind, but I do like to fly a good kite now and then, especially with my kids. It has been rumored that the wind has been known to blow on occasion at Thanksgiving Point.

GOLF AT THANKSGIVING POINT

Artist's Note

I have one goal when I golf, and that is to finish with the same people I started with. The towels on the grass are actually beach towels to represent the amount of time many of us spend in the sand. The course at Thanksgiving Point was designed by Johnny Miller which makes for some real championship play if you are up to it.

FARM COUNTRY

Artist's Note

Of all the structures at Thanksgiving Point, I love the big red barn most. It represents Americana architecture on a grand scale. The big red barn to me reminds me so much of the hard work our pioneers went through as they farmed this land, then and now. If you ever have the chance to attend an event inside the show barn, it will be time well spent.

BEYOND UTAH'S BORDERS

"The aim of art is to represent not the outward
appearance of things, but their inward significance."

Aristotle

Artist's Note

Home is where I hang my hat and Utah is that home. However, I love to see the world and the way others live—their culture, values, traditions, food, and fun. I feel compelled to capture in my art as much of the human experience as I can. "Folk art," by definition, means "people art." No matter where I travel I try to portray the stories of the people and their love of home and country. That's my job and I love it.

WHEN THE SAINTS CROSSED THE PLAINS TO COME TO UTAH, THE GOAL WAS TO FIND ISOLATION FROM THE REST OF THE WORLD.

Today, the goal in Utah has changed. Utah seeks to be part of the global community. Utah extends its hand of friendship, not only to every state in the Union, but to every country in the world.

Throughout the years, Utah has welcomed into its communities immigrants and refugees from every corner of the earth. There isn't a foreign language that isn't spoken in Utah. When the 2002 Olympics came to Utah, every visiting athlete was welcomed and assisted by someone speaking their native tongue. Often that person was a direct descendent of immigrants from the visiting country.

Utah feels a direct connection with the lands of its forefathers. Utah works to provide global trade opportunities for its businesses and factories. When tragedies occur in any part of the world, trains, planes, and trucks are loaded with relief supplies to assist the needy. Cultural exchange is welcomed and diverse opinions and ideas are invited as part of the Utah political discussion.

Utah is no longer a secluded society of refugees. It is an active participant in the global picture. Yet it retains its heritage. And that is an important part of Utah's appeal and beauty.

Eric in his studio painting "Festival of Trees."

AUTHOR'S NOTE

F A PICTURE PAINTS A THOUSAND WORDS, THEN WHY AM I WRITING ANYTHING IN THIS BOOK?

I have known Eric Dowdle for many years, even before he began painting in the folk art syle. I have also known him well enough to give him brutal, if not unfair, criticism of his work. I do this mostly in fun and to keep an artist humble. I am, in truth, probably his biggest fan.

When he asked me to write a book on Utah that would feature his Utah paintings, I realized that most people would want to look at his amazing work more than read anything that could be written. In deferance to that fact, I have tried to keep my descriptions of Utah short yet interesting as a suitable frame for each painting.

I would like to thank Eric for providing, in addition to his original art, his own perspective on each piece in the *Artist's Notes* sections of each chapter.

Many people who love Eric's art stepped up to help on this book.

First and formost, I would like to thank Eric's family, especially his lovely wife Deb, who was a principle editor of this book. Also his brother Mark who offered encouragement, support, and pointed me to one of my editors, Cathi Darrington, who has been very helpful and encouraging. And thanks to Eric's children, Autumn, Joey, Ryan, Shawn, and Cody who would patiently wait while I regularly borrowed their dad for pointers on layout and content.

This book would not have been possible without Eric's staff at Dowdle Folk Art. They assisted in assembling all of the necessary components to keep this project going. It has been, in many ways, like putting together one of Eric's jigsaw puzzles that are so incredibly popular throughout Utah.

And lastly, I would like to thank Lane and Joy Beattie for their appropriate forword for this book. They know Deb and Eric well and their support was very encouraging as we worked on this showpiece of Utah and Eric's art.

William Kurtis